Tiger Features

Sharon Callen

Tigers have their own creature features.

They have four strong legs and four padded feet.

fur

claws

Tigers have sharp claws and striped fur.

4

teeth

A tiger has 30 sharp teeth.

Tigers can run.

It's a Fact

Tigers can run at 35 miles per hour.

Tiger Features

legs	4
feet	padded
fur	striped
teeth	30